This book belongs to:

If found, please contact:

41274653R00062

Made in the USA
San Bernardino, CA
01 July 2019